"Top producers today realize they can no longer get by on product expertise alone. They know the real expert is the customer."

"The deeper the dialogue, the greater the sales results."

The Sales Success Handbook:

20 Lessons to Open and Close Sales Now

LINDA RICHARDSON

MCGRAW-HILL
New York Chicago San Francisco Lisbon
London Madrid Mexico City Milan New Delhi
San Juan Seoul Singapore Sydney Toronto

The **McGraw·Hill** Companies

5 6 7 8 9 0 DOC/DOC 0 9 8 7 6 5 4

ISBN 0-07-141636-6

Editorial and Production services provided by CWL Publishing Enterprises,
Madison, WI, www.cwlpub.com.

This book is printed on recycled, acid-free paper containing a mini-
mum of 50% recycled, de-inked fiber.

McGraw-Hill books are available at special quantity discounts to use as
premiums and sales promotions, or for use in corporate training programs. For
more information, please write to the Director of Special Sales, Professional
Publishing, McGraw-Hill, Two Penn Plaza, New York, NY 10121-2298. Or
contact your local bookstore.

To order
*The Sales Success
Handbook*
call 1-800-842-3075

Contents

☑ *Sales talk*

Sales talk. What is it? It is more than you talking. Sales talk takes two. It is not a monologue. It is a dialogue. It is a customer-centered exchange of information that begins and ends with the customer whose needs must drive the conversation.

You have a sales approach you use consciously or unconsciously every day. How open are you to looking at your sales talk up close? If you are open, these lessons can help you assess yourself, spot your strengths and weaknesses, and change your sales talk. You will tap into your natural skills, leverage your knowledge, and sell more by creating compelling dialogues with your customers.

You are probably thinking, "But I already do all that." And it is likely that you do. But how are you keeping up with the changes that are occurring everywhere around you—with your customers, your competitors, your markets, and your own organization?

Relying solely on product knowledge or technical expertise doesn't work in today's environment. The Internet is a free and convenient source of knowledge, giving customers more information than ever before. Salespeople face a tough business climate in which they need to win all the good deals that are out there. In this environment, products—once the key differentiator—are the equalizer. Instead of talking about products, your role is to communicate a message in which you add value, provide perspective, and show how your features and benefits apply to and satisfy customer needs.

Most salespeople use a model for selling that has been the predominant model for decades. It primarily relies on the old, tried-but-

no-longer-true feature-and-benefit focus. Too many salespeople tell their product stories too soon, without necessarily meaning to do so, and invariably talk from a generic product vs. customer point of view. When they ask about needs, they don't go far enough. When they identify a need, they *jump* to product, rather than *create a rich dialogue* to understand why, how, or when.

Selling today is more demanding. As business becomes more challenging, salespeople need a higher level of skill. My experience, in more than two decades of working with tens of thousands of salespeople in some of the finest organizations in the world, shows that at *best* only 30% of salespeople truly practice need-based consultative selling and no more than one third of those achieve trusted-advisor level with their customers.

The bottom line is that too many salespeople are still too quick to tell a product story. While most *think solution*, they *present product.* Because they tend to talk more than they listen, they create an imbalanced give/get ratio instead of a 50/50 dialogue. Overall, the level of preparation and questioning does not measure up. Most sales organizations have good salespeople, but they lack enough superb salespeople to drive the growth they need to succeed.

As much as everything else is changing, the old formulas of selling features and benefits are still around, blocking dialogues and holding good salespeople back from becoming superb.

The lessons in *The Sales Success Handbook* will let you tap into your natural talents by helping you take advantage of your personal strengths, build on them, and create Sales talk that sells.

"Check your sales talk. Measure your 'give/get ratio.'"

☑ *Create a dialogue*

---

*I*f you were to ask 100 salespeople you know whether their approach was *customer*-centered or *product*-centered, what would they say? Few, if any, would boast about selling "a box."

Most salespeople believe that they know their customers' needs. They believe they are positioning solutions, not products. They believe they are customer-focused. These beliefs are the biggest obstacles keeping them from making the changes they need to make in their Sales talk.

Selling styles run the gamut. There is a sales style continuum. At one end of the continuum is generic product selling, basically a monologue, a "product dump." At the other end is consultative selling, an interactive *dialogue* that focuses on the specific needs of the customer. 100% on either end is impossible. All salespeople are somewhere in between.

Some salespeople are charismatic sellers who rely on their interpersonal skills and charm. Others are technical experts, substantive in content but weak in customer focus. There are the "killers," always rushing to the close, often at the expense of the relationship. These characterizations of sales types are extreme, but they set the context for thinking about how salespeople approach sales.

The majority of salespeople today use a combination of approaches. They want to be liked, they want to be credible, they want to close, *and* they want to meet the needs of their customers. But for most salespeople, this amalgamation has resulted in a *quasi-consultative* approach at best. While quasi-consultative salespeople identify customer needs and are productive, they fall short of what they could accomplish.

Salespeople who are at the consultative end of the continuum create efficient but robust dialogues with their customers that enable them to connect and learn more with each conversation. The dialogues are active, with balanced exchanges between the salesperson and the customer. What they do looks easy and sounds like common sense, but it is far from simple and it is not common practice.

The line between quasi-consultative selling and consultative selling is fine, but if all other factors are basically equal, the line means the difference between winning business or losing to a competitor. It can be the difference between being viewed as a technical specialist and being a trusted advisor. With relatively equal competitors, it is the sales talk of the salesperson or sales team that makes the difference between winning and losing business.

Here are ways you can create a robust dialogue:

Assess your sales talk: How interactive are your sales dialogues? What is your give/get ratio?

Commit to do something different: Ask more probing questions.

Stop thinking in terms of educating customers: Think more about educating yourself about your customers.

"Increase your sales dialogue to increase your sales results."

☑ *Always be preparing*

---

*T*op performers treat preparation differently. They are always preparing—*before* and *after* each customer meeting.

How do you prepare? Do you think to yourself—what does my customer need, what can I position that will make it easy for my customer to say yes? Do you let ideas percolate in your mind so you can be creative and proactive?

Having a preparation strategy will *shorten* your preparation time and increase the impact. As you prepare, follow these three steps:

- Begin with **strategic preparation**. Think about your longer-term relationship objectives and then set your short-term immediate objective for the call. Make sure your objective is measurable, is achievable, and has a time frame so you can maintain momentum, assess the outcome of your call, and accelerate your close. Visualize the flow of your call and build in time for the customer to talk.
- Next, do **customer preparation**. Think about your customer's objectives, situation, needs, and decision criteria.
- Finally, focus on your **product/technical preparation**. Use your range of products and capabilities to meet your customer's needs. Plan the questions you will ask, anticipate objections, and customize your materials.

Most salespeople prepare backwards. They start with product/technical preparation. Beginning with strategic preparation will help you save time by letting you target your efforts and remain customer-focused.

To help you in your preparation, stay up to date on industry and company news. Leverage your team for ideas. Review your customer files so that you can build on any information you already have and avoid unnecessary repetition. Prepare the materials you think you will need and tailor whatever you plan to give to the customer to make sure it applies to the customer.

As you visualize your agenda for the call, make sure you remain customer-focused. Prior to the call, whenever possible, get customer input on your agenda. But even when you get input, always check your agenda to get the feedback you need to get buy-in, make adjustments, and go forward.

Here are tips to help you prepare:

Prepare for all customer calls: Set a measurable objective with a time frame for each call to help you maintain momentum and accelerate your close.

Tailor all material: Show your customer your focus is on his or her needs.

Visualize your call: Plan the flow of your call and build in time for the customer to talk.

"In preparing put first things first. Start with your objective."

☑ *Sharpen your critical skills*

*T*op performers often say that their sales dialogues feel more like brainstorming with their customers than "selling." These are the six critical skills that are fundamental to making their dialogues so fluid and productive:

- Presence—communicating energy, conviction, and interest when speaking and listening
- Relating—building rapport, using acknowledgment, and expressing empathy to connect with customers
- Questioning—creating a logical questioning strategy and effectively using probing skills to uncover needs
- Listening—understanding what the customer communicates in words, tone, and body language
- Positioning—persuasively demonstrating value and application to the customer by customizing your product knowledge to the needs of the customer
- Checking—eliciting feedback on what you have said to gauge customer understanding and agreement

These skills are the tools of selling. The sharper the skills, the more effective the salesperson. A weakness in any one of the skills puts a cap on effectiveness. For example, if the salesperson can't establish rapport with the customer, it is unlikely the customer will open up in answering questions. If the salesperson is a poor listener, answers lose their value. And without an understanding of customer needs, it's almost impossible to connect capabilities to customer needs.

Dialogue selling requires product knowledge and technical expertise, but equal to these is customer knowledge and skill. In dialogue selling, the salesperson becomes a resource person who, because he or she fully understands that particular customer's specific needs, can meet the needs that relate to his or her product and also cross-sell and meet the customer's broader spectrum of needs. To succeed in dialogue selling, you must master the six critical skills.

Here are ways you can sharpen these skills:

Assess your six critical skills: presence, relating, questioning, listening, positioning, checking. Force-rank the skills. Identify your strengths and areas for improvement. Work on one skill at a time to get it to the next level.

Commit to self-critique: At the end of each call, critique your skills as well as the content of the meeting.

Ask for feedback: Elicit feedback from your customers and colleagues.

"Salespeople are made, not born. For most salespeople, sales excellence does not just come naturally."

☑ *Open with a focus on your customer*

*T*he opening of the call sets the tone. There are four important things to accomplish as you open: establish rapport with the customer, clarify the purpose of the meeting, set the focus on the customer, and bridge to needs. Where you are in the sales cycle determines the emphasis on each. But even in the quickest follow-up telephone call, the best salespeople fully leverage their openings.

Don't skimp on building rapport. Take the time as you prepare to plan your rapport while staying alert to cues for spontaneous rapport, such as photos or other, more personal signals. Be sensitive to customers who are not open to rapport at that moment.

After you have established rapport, state the *purpose* of your call from your *customer's perspective.* Briefly bullet the key items of your agenda and check with the customer that the agenda meets his or her expectations.

While your objective is the measurable action step you want to achieve, your purpose answers the all-important question, *"What's in it for the customer?"* Aim for your objective, but position your purpose as you open to engage and gain the interest of the customer. Consider the following two openings:

Opening 1: You state your *objective:* "Bill, John said you might be interested in the new things we are doing in research with …, so I'm here to talk with you about our …." The spotlight is on *you* and you are moving to *discuss product.*

Opening 2: You state your *purpose.* "Bill, thanks for taking the time to meet with me ... (rapport). I know how busy you are and I appreciate the time. John said you are doing some interesting things in .... I've given thought to that and looked at your new Web site, which looks great. I'd like to learn more about what you are doing in ... and then explore how we might ... (briefly bullet your agenda). How does that sound?" The spotlight is on the *customer* and you are positioned to *identify needs.*

Opening 1 is headed toward a generic product discussion, while Opening 2 is leading to an interactive dialogue to understand the customer's objective and needs *before* you cover your capabilities or ideas.

During the meeting, get credit for your preparation. Leverage that you are prepared by positioning the homework you have done to increase your credibility (as in Opening 2).

Many salespeople are self-focused as they open, which actually hurts not only rapport but also the relationship. The customer-focused salesperson realizes the importance of an opening that builds common ground and a shared understanding of the customer's needs.

Here are some tips for optimizing your opening:

Prepare for rapport: Take the time to plan how you will build rapport.

Fully leverage your opening: Plan your opening from what you want to accomplish— your greeting, rapport, purpose/agenda, and checking of the agenda.

Define your purpose: Translate your measurable objective into your customer-focused *purpose* to gain the interest of the customer.

"There are three rules for a good opening: rapport, rapport, and rapport."

☑ *Relate to your customers*

*T*he critical skills of questioning, listening, positioning, and checking are the *know*-how skills. But the skill of *relating*—which includes rapport, acknowledgment, and empathy—is the *feel*-how skill. Building rapport is often connected to the opening of a call. But there are also other powerful ways and times to relate throughout the call.

Many salespeople get into sales because they "like people." As critically important as rapport is, it is only one part of relating to customers. Rapport is the "like people," chitchat part of relating. Many salespeople who are good at rapport limit their ability to connect with customers to that part of relating. They don't reap the benefits of using acknowledgment and empathy throughout the dialogue.

In a training session, a group of salespeople were confronted with an objection exercise in which an irate senior-level customer said, "Your people are always spouting formulas as if we know what to do with them!" They were asked to respond with empathy.

They said, "What is it you don't understand?" and "I'll go over the process again" and so on. No one initially came up with an empathy statement. It took a while to arrive at "We certainly don't mean to do that. I'm sorry we have not been clear. What specifically …?"

Acknowledgment and empathy are powerful skills. Although questions can be empathetic in tone, questions don't replace empathy or acknowledgment. For example, if a customer mentions a problem, a good salesperson might ask, "How did you handle that?" A superb salesperson is likely to introduce the question with empathy to convey concern and, most important, encourage a more complete response—for example, "I'm sorry to hear that that happened," followed by the question. Both acknowledgment and empathy are very important to an active dialogue. Empathy goes a step beyond acknowledgment in showing concern for the customer and, when used effectively, it can help form personal bonds.

Empathy is not easy for some salespeople to express. They may feel empathy, but are not comfortable communicating it. Verbally expressing concern and caring can help you reduce customer defenses and make you more persuasive. Especially when a customer is emotional or the topic is sensitive, it is very helpful to respond *first* with an expression of genuine empathy, to make the customer more receptive to your response. Empathy needs to be genuine, because phony empathy is usually transparent to today's savvy customers.

Many salespeople are more comfortable using acknowledgment because it is more neutral. Using acknowledgment is also an effective way to connect with customers.

Here's how to broaden your relating skills:

Acknowledge, acknowledge, acknowledge: Verbally indicate you heard what the customer has said.

Empathize: Express genuine empathy when your customer is disturbed, excited, or emotional.

Rapport: Develop your rapport skills by preparing how you will build rapport. Rapport is the first step in building a relationship.

"Acknowledgment is the oxygen of sales."

☑ *Position your questioning*

***M**any* salespeople think that after their opening they are ready to start "selling." While their goal may be to understand customer needs, too many go straight to talking product—true to a traditional feature-and-benefit formula. Even when salespeople move to asking questions, they can do so in a way that does not inspire customer buy-in. By asking questions without any setup, they can limit the level of cooperation they get.

Instead, as you wrap up your opening, bridge to customer needs by setting the expectation that you will be asking questions and check to get the customer's agreement. The reason to do this is that when people are made a part of the decision, it is more likely they will participate actively and enthusiastically. If you preface the reason you'd like to ask questions with a customer benefit, you will increase the cooperation you get. For example, "I've looked at ... in preparation for our meeting .... To help me focus on your interests, may I ask ...?" It is also important to preface your preparation to show the effort you have made to make the meeting meaningful.

Even with customers who say, "Tell me about X product" or "What do you have for me today?" don't succumb to the temptation of product before needs. Say, "Yes. I've put together some material on .... So I can focus the discussion on what is important to you, may I ask a few questions? What ...? Can you tell me ...?" If it is later in the sales cycle and you have already identified needs, recap those needs and ask a question to identify additional needs or concerns and to learn if anything has changed so that you can incorporate that into the dialogue.

Knowing when you are exiting your opening and creating a bridge to needs will help you move into a robust need dialogue. It will also help you avoid getting to product too soon.

Here are a few ideas to help you create a bridge to needs as you exit your opening:

Reference your homework: Build credibility by reinforcing that you are prepared but that you also would like to ask questions.

Bridge to customer needs: Begin by sharing your reason for asking questions, to encourage the customer to participate in the dialogue.

Focus on a customer benefit: Let the customer know how he or she will benefit by participating in the dialogue.

"Pave the way for the need dialogue."

☑ *Develop a questioning strategy*

*E*ven when customers share their needs because they are open or because you've asked questions, don't let the dialogue fall short of fully understanding needs. By having a logical questioning strategy, you can create a dialogue that will let you efficiently and effectively explore the needs of your customers.

Your questioning strategy gives you a *structure* to develop a dialogue rich in needs and your questioning skills give you the flexibility you need within the structure to improvise while still directing the dialogue. Since you are likely to be asking more questions, planning the overall structure and flow of your questions is essential.

Your questioning strategy will enable you to create effective and efficient *need dialogues* with your customers. As you plan your questioning strategy, begin broadly. Start by asking about the customer's *objectives*. An understanding of what the customer wants to accomplish provides the *best foundation* for probing more deeply. It is astounding how many salespeople skip this question.

Once you have a clear understanding of the customer's *objectives*, then ask about the *current situation*. Probe this to learn about priorities and concerns. Next, ask about *level of satisfaction* and drill down to understand what is working and what needs to be changed. As appropriate, also ask about *future needs*, so you can take them into consideration to help you differentiate your solution. As appropriate, tactfully ask about personal needs so you can build *personal motivators* into your solution and be more persuasive. Throughout your questioning strategy, look for opportunities to drill down to learn more.

Once you have a full understanding of needs (customer's objective, current situation, level of satisfaction, future needs), ask *implementation questions* that have not been addressed in the course of the dialogue. Critical to your being able to realistically assess the opportunity and close are questions about *implementation,* including budget, timeframe, compelling event driving the decision, decision-making process (including decision makers and influencers), competitors, relationships, and other related initiatives.

Here are some ways to use a questioning strategy:

Implement a powerful question strategy to create high-impact need dialogues: Begin with more strategic questions. Learn about the current situation. Learn about level of satisfaction. Identify future and personal needs. Drill down as appropriate.

Prepare your questions: Questions are too important to leave to chance. Yet you should remain spontaneous. Within your questioning structure, listen for opportunities to drill down, learn more, and pick up on customer cues.

Ask about implementation: Understand budget, timeframe, compelling event, decision makers, competitors, and related initiatives.

"A questioning strategy gives you a way to create a true need dialogue."

☐ Think answers

☑ *Think questions*

*W*hen you ask most salespeople why they are meeting with a customer, the word "tell" dominates their responses. When a salesperson called his product specialist to help him compose an e-mail to a hot prospect and asked for help in describing the purpose of the meeting they would be requesting, the specialist said, "To meet with you to tell you about our fully integrated ... and how we can ..." A customer-first mindset would have changed the nuance of the e-mail. A specialist tuned into his or her sales talk might have said, "To learn about your ... initiative and discuss how our fully integrated ... might support you in ...." The shift is small—but powerful.

Certainly it makes sense to want to "tell"—provided that what you tell is persuasive. A questioning mindset is about perspective. When you think about approaching customers, do you think answers or questions? There is a time and a place for answers. But without a questioning mindset, you may find yourself answering before either you or the customer are ready.

While it makes perfect sense to think questions, most salespeople have developed the opposite habit. Many are reluctant to ask questions, for many reasons. They think:

- *"There isn't enough time."* The time spent asking questions will help you develop a winning solution and often will save you time by allowing you to focus on what is important to the customer.
- *"I'll lose control."* The person who controls the questions generally controls the call.

"The customer will think I'm unprepared." Customers can evaluate you by the quality of your questions. The right questions show how well prepared you are, especially if you position them by referring to your preparation. For example, "I spoke with John before our meeting and he was helpful in providing .... I've .... I would like to hear from your perspective your vision of how ...."

- *"Customers will object."* If you preface your questions well by showing a level of understanding and preparation, most customers will welcome questions rather than a product dump.

- *"I don't want to risk offending my customer."* It is more often salespeople than customers who feel uncomfortable about questioning. Effective questioning skills can help offset this reluctance.

- *"Questions will raise negative issues."* When negative issues are on the table, you have a chance to resolve them.

- *"I'm experienced and already know ...."* Making assumptions without checking, validating, or learning more can easily cost the deal.

- *"My job is to have the answer."* If customers wanted only product answers, this would be true. But customers want value and perspective. They want your answer to apply to them.

Here are some guidelines to help you think questions:

Put customer needs first: This means questions before answers.

Hold back your instinct to answer: It's natural that you want to tell. Hold back, not indefinitely, but just long enough to tailor your response.

Ask one more question: Push yourself to learn one more thing.

"The question mark is the most important punctuation mark in sales grammar."

☑ *Develop deeper need dialogues*

*H*ow do you respond when a customer makes a comment, asks a question, or objects? Most salespeople respond with an answer—but there are alternatives.

When a customer tells you something, don't immediately respond with an answer. Instead of being the answer man or answer woman, acknowledge the comment and, when appropriate, find out more by asking a "Why?" question. Take a moment to show your thoughtful consideration.

Consider this simple situation. The customer asks, "Does this come in a more neutral color?" The average salesperson is likely to respond with an answer.

- "Yes. It comes in ...." (product before need)
- "No. Only one color ...." (giving up before needs are identified)
- "But it's the latest color." (contradiction)
- "Oh, so what you are saying is you don't like the color?" (reflective listening)
- "If I can get it in ... color, then will you buy it?" ("if/then" technique that moves to the close before the needs or obstacles are understood)
- "Well, the quality is ...." or "What do you think of the fabric?" (changing the platform)
- "Oh, is the color too bright?" (interpretation, translation, assumption/putting words in the customer's mouth)

- "Most customers feel it is very neutral." (discounting the objection)
- "Some of my other customers feel the same way." (reinforcing the objection)
- "Well, I'm not sure if you'd like a darker color, but we also offer ...." (telling vs. checking)

In each response, the salesperson is trying to persuade or evade. But without connecting (acknowledgment) and getting more information (question), the responses are defensive and/or self-centered vs. customer-centered. By using acknowledgment and a question, the salesperson could have connected, learned more, and been more persuasive. For example:

The tendency to answer is deeply entrenched in most salespeople. The customer who asks, "Why does it take two months? That seems so long," may be satisfied with "Because we tailor the packaging." However, you can be the salesperson who connects better and closes more sales by saying, "Two months can seem long. May I ask what your concern is about the two-month delivery?" Even if the two months cannot be adjusted, your sales talk is customer-centered and shows a willingness to meet the needs of the customer.

Here are some tips to efficiently create effective need dialogues:

Slow down: Don't be so fast to offer an answer.

Use acknowledgment: Introduce your questions by acknowledging what the customer has said (not paraphrasing), to encourage the customer to answer.

Be curious: Find out why.

"Effective questioning is half the job of sales."

☐ Focus on the questions you ask

☑ *Focus on how skillfully you ask questions*

Of course, most salespeople ask questions—but what is the quality, the range, and the impact of those questions?

Sales questions are critical. Begin by *planning* the questions you will ask. If you are not sure *what* questions to ask, check with a manager, a colleague, or a specialist.

How you ask questions is as important as *what* you ask. Asking questions effectively takes skill, discipline, knowledge, and confidence. You don't want to sound like a prosecuting attorney.

As you develop your questions, think about the structure, the pace, and the tactics you will use to get your customers to talk and open up.

How you phrase, position, and sequence your questions will have an impact on how willing your customer is to participate in the dialogue and what you are able to learn. Compare these two questions: "Who makes the decision?" and "Once you have reviewed this, what will your decision process involve?" The first question will prompt a customer to give a short and possibly incomplete, misleading response. The second question, because it already recognizes the customer's role, is likely to prompt a more accurate and informative reply.

Preface your questions to encourage a robust dialogue. As a lead-in to your questions, to motivate the customer to share information, preface with *acknowledgment:* for example, *"I understand that it is time-consuming.* How are you handling it now?" For more sensitive or emotional situations, you can preface with *empathy:* for example, *"I'm very sorry for the disruption this is causing.* What happened?" You can also preface questions with a *customer benefit,* such as "So I can take the needs of the regions into consideration, how does the local ...?" Trading is another excellent way to preface, by exchanging information: "Our specialists tell us there is a slowdown in .... How is that impacting your plans?"

Here are some tips to strengthen how you ask questions:

Structure your questions: Develop the habit of asking open-ended vs. closed-ended questions to create a robust dialogue. Closed-ended questions begin with words such as "Do" and "Are" and result in yes-or-no answers.

Pace your questions: Ask one question at a time rather than multiple questions together. When confronted with several questions at once, the customer is unlikely to answer all questions or provide complete answers. Avoid answering your own questions or providing multiple-choice answers. Ask a question and then be silent.

Ask drill-down questions: After the customer responds, drill down with a question to gain more insight and information. Drill-down questions help you gain more information by letting you explore what the customer has said.

"Give as much thought to how you ask your questions as to what you ask."

☐ Listen efficiently

☑ *Listen effectively*

---

*L*istening in sales requires the equivalent of a zoom lens. *Effective* listening is not the same as *efficient* listening. Effective listening enables you to show interest, connect with the customer, and gain a fuller understanding of the customer's needs.

Most salespeople listen *efficiently*. They listen to what they think is important. They listen with an ear to talk vs. absorb and assess. While a small percentage of salespeople may zone out, most salespeople do listen efficiently—they pay enough attention to stay active in the dialogue.

Listening *effectively* goes beyond this. Effective listeners not only stay in the dialogue but also pay attention with a high level of intensity. They listen to *all* content and also observe the tone of voice, pacing, and emphasis. They maintain good eye contact and/or acknowledge. They listen with an ear to *question* and *integrate*. They observe body language and test the customer's verbal message against what they read. Their follow-up questions tell the customer they are listening. They are sensitive to the messages they communicate with their own body language.

Another way they show they are listening is by taking notes judiciously of *all* key important information. Taking notes seems to be a lost art, but great notes are essential to truly customizing solutions and are invaluable in creating winning proposals and following up flawlessly.

Listening is one of the six critical skills essential to an effective dialogue. In fact, when we ask top salespeople about their skills and how they sell, the majority rate listening as their strongest skill.

Ambiguous words can hold the key to understanding the customer's needs and criteria for making decisions. Listen for words or ideas to explore or clarify to avoid talking at cross-purposes. By clarifying what broad words mean and getting more information, you can tailor how you discuss your solutions to transform what could have been a generic response to a tailored and persuasive one.

For example, if a customer says, "Frankly, I was pretty *impressed* with your competitor," you can gain invaluable information if you ask, "I know you were speaking to X. What impressed you, specifically?" If the customer says, "It's too *rich* for us," ask, "Rich? How so?" If the customer says, "I have *hesitations* about X," ask, "I know you want to feel comfortable going forward. What's causing you to hesitate?" If a customer says, "You are not *consistent*," acknowledge and find out in what way. *Impressed, rich, hesitations,* and *consistent* are words to clarify.

Here are some strategies to help you listen effectively rather than efficiently:

Listen for content: Train your ear to hear what is important to the customer and clarify and explore all ambiguous words.

Listen for emphasis and emotions: Words that the customer underscores with his or her voice or delivers emotionally you should note and explore. Emotional words can give insights into more personal needs.

Use body language: Listen with your eyes as well as your ears. Read your customer's body language to gain insight into how he or she feels about something—confused, disturbed, elated, involved, or detached. Check to validate.

"Listen to learn. The best salespeople are the best listeners."

☑ *Position your message*

*P*ositioning, one of the six critical skills, allows you to relate your capabilities to your customers' needs. The way to position is to tell your story—but it must be more than a product story. It is the opposite of a generic product pitch.

Product knowledge is just the foundation here. Having a strong message and knowing how to customize it to incorporate your customer's needs is critical in winning business.

The first level of positioning is developing a core message that is clear, customer-focused, and graphic. You must know what you want to communicate and use words and images that the customer can understand and relate to.

The second level of positioning is to integrate customer needs into a message tailored for a specific customer. You use your critical and creative skills to understand the customer's needs, language, and perspective and to create the link to your offerings.

To position your message:

- Integrate and begin with a concise recap of the needs ("We've discussed your objective to ...")
- Concisely and graphically position the tailored features and benefits of your recommendation ("Based on our discussion to ... we can ... so you can ...")
- Finally, ask a checking question to get feedback ("How does that sound?")

There is a third level to positioning. As you learn more during the sales process, incorporate into your message what you've learned and

23

what is happening as you move through the sales cycle. For example, if you present a proposal to key influencers, you should then incorporate what you learn there and *reposition* your message when you present to the expanded group of influencers and decision makers.

You can use positioning throughout the dialogue, whenever you want to be persuasive. Here are a couple of examples:

- When asking a question to gain access—"You've been very helpful in our understanding .... When I was speaking with our specialist .... We'd like to meet with the head of IT and you so we can build your strategy into our presentation" (vs. "We'd like to meet with your head of IT")
- When discussing your capabilities—"Our ... will enable you to get your data to your 30 division heads globally before the ... so you can ..." (vs. "Our ... lets us deliver ... by ...").

The value of positioning is that it shows customer focus and customer knowledge.

Here are strategies to help you position your message persuasively:

Know the message you want to communicate: Practice how you will describe your capabilities. Make sure your core message is customer-focused, concise, and graphic.

Update your message continuously: Reflect changes in your company's and your customer's situation, needs, and perceptions.

Position effectively: Summarize key customer benefits concisely, to lead into your message or recommendation; integrate into your core message the specific customer needs you have uncovered, concisely and graphically.

"'The medium is the message.'—You are the medium for your company's message."

☑ *Analyze your competitors*

*Y*ou will almost always face tough competition. It is your job to know your competitors and create a competitive strategy. Regardless of how much market intelligence you have about the competitors from your research or your marketing team (and often it's not as much as you would like), it is equally critical to understand how your customer feels about the competitors, so that you can effectively position against them—and do it in a way that neither denigrates nor promotes them.

As a part of your preparation, learn as much as possible about your competitors using the Internet, files, colleagues, literature, trade shows, annual reports, competitors, and advertisements.

One source of competitive information often not tapped is customers. Most customers will answer questions like "Who else are you speaking with?" "How do you feel about them?" "What has been your experience?" "What do you like about working with them?" "What would you change?" "What is their approach?" "Who do you work with there?" "How do we compare?" As you listen, don't become defensive. Don't denigrate the competition. Directly criticizing a competitor reflects badly on you. You might even be insulting the customer who selected the competitor. Instead, ask targeted questions and help the customer make comparisons.

Find out what your competitors are offering, what the relationship history is, and who your competitors have access to. Find out how your customers feel about your competitors and ask how you stack up. Determine how your level of access to the customer and other members of the customer's decision-making team compares.

Asking questions about the competition saves time—and deals. When one salesperson asked how his proposal stacked up, he was told he was number two. Why? The software package. With this information, he teamed up with a software firm and submitted a revised proposal that won.

With competitive data, you can create a competitive strategy, bolster how and what you sell, and better position yourself against the competition. You will also gain competitive feedback that you can funnel to your organization to spur new products, product improvements, and more effective competitive strategies. By knowing your competitors, you will be able to to diffuse any "mines" again you that your competitors plant.

Here are some tips on offsetting competitors:

Know your competitors: Develop data about your competitors and use it to position against them.

Get your customer's perspective: Your customers are a great source of competitive information. Find out how they view competitors compared with their perceptions of you.

Tactfully highlight competitive weaknesses: When you have a competitive strength or know about a weakness of a competitor, before you express your view, ask a question that focuses your customer on the competitor's weakness. Then position your strengths.

"Know your competitors' strengths and weaknesses and how you stack up."

✓ Use objections to move forward

*C*ustomers object for many reasons. Objections can be frustrating, but they are also a healthy sign in that your customer is listening critically and considering your proposition.

Objections provide a great way for you to build credibility and move forward in the sale. However, most salespeople don't handle objections strategically. Instead they get defensive and try to argue with the customer, which just makes the customer defensive in return. Another common response to objections is just the opposite of defensiveness: salespeople give up.

An alternative to "fight" or "flight" responses is to use acknowledgment and questions to understand the objection and obtain the information needed to resolve the objection.

How you respond to key objections ultimately determines whether an objection is a negative or a positive force in the sale, whether it closes down the opportunity or leads to the close.

Traditional methods for dealing with objections give the salesperson the awesome task of changing the customer's mind. But the best way to think about an objection is that *you* need more information. Using acknowledgment and question(s) engaging the customer in a collaborative effort to solve the problem.

When a top salesperson in one of the most highly regarded sales organizations in the world was asked his secret for success, he replied, "Empathy." Acknowledgment and empathy are critical throughout the sales dialogue and are particularly useful in resolving objections.

Acknowledgment says to your customer, "I understand what you have said." Empathy says, "I care." Acknowledgment is highly appropriate throughout the dialogue, but especially with objections. Empathy is appropriate when the customer is upset or the situation is more troublesome, personal, serious, or emotional. Both show you care about the customer's feelings.

In resolving objections, appreciate that most customers know more about their needs than you do. By maintaining the connection with acknowledgment or empathy and learning more about the objection through questioning, you will avoid making assumptions, becoming defensive, or giving up.

To help turn objections into opportunities:

Acknowledge or show empathy for the customer's concerns: Reframe the negative situation by verbalizing that you understand the objection (not paraphrasing). The acknowledgment or empathy will pave the way for you to narrow down the concern with a question so that you can effectively address it. Don't erase your acknowledgment or empathy by using the word "but."

Ask questions to learn more about the objection: Objections are usually broad and need to be clarified.

Position your response: Be concise, be specific, and customize your response to meet the customer's needs. Then check for feedback: ask a question to find out how well you have satisfied the objection.

"General objections only get general answers."

☑ *Check for customer feedback*

*C*hecking, one of the six critical skills, is the process of asking your customer how he or she feels about what you have said *before* either of you move on to another point. Although it's important to summarize needs concisely and accurately, summaries do not provide what you can get from checking. Many salespeople recap (tell); far fewer check (ask).

Checking for feedback is an essential skill for salespeople who *really* want to *know* where they stand in meeting customer needs. It helps you gauge how you are progressing and gives you the information you need to navigate the sale and make adjustments. It keeps you from assuming that the customer understands or accepts what you have said. (Silence from the customer does not mean agreement.)

It keeps the call interactive: continuously asking for feedback keeps your customer involved, active, and interested. Most important, feedback from checking lets you refine your message and makes you more confident to close because you understand how the customer is likely to respond.

Checking also helps you identify obstacles and opportunities so you can address them. For example, during the dialogue you might ask the customer, "Which sounds better at first glance, X or Y?" and "What system do you have?" These questions will let you save time, focus the dialogue, and help you tailor your message.

Each time you position a major point of your message, answer a question, or respond to an objection, check for feedback to gauge the customer's reaction. If the customer understands and agrees, your checking question will save you time, because you'll know that you don't have to address that point further. If feedback from your checking shows the customer still has a question, you can backtrack, ask questions yourself, make adjustments, and/or reset your objective.

Checking is the skill that salespeople resist the most—initially. They see it as risky because the feedback may be negative—objections, complaints, requests, demands. But with practice, they find that checking is indispensable—a virtual secret weapon.

Don't confuse checking with high-pressure or manipulative tactics. Checking is neither. Checking questions are open-ended—*what, how, to what extent*. They are not leading questions like "Don't you want to save money?" or "Don't you agree this benefits you?" Leading questions force the customer to say yes and be pushed to buy. Checking is different, because it seeks all feedback.

Checking is the opposite of summarizing. Summarizing *gives* information: for example, "I think X will work well in your structure because it meets your objective to ...." Checking *gets* information: for example, "How do you think X will work in your structure to meet your objective to ...?" After all, it is not what *you* think that counts, but what the *customer* thinks.

Here are some key strategies to check for feedback:

Check for feedback before moving on: Ask for feedback on all important information you position.

Use checking questions throughout the call: Get customer feedback from your opening to your close.

Do a reality check on your objective: Continuous checking lets you assess how realistic your sales objective is and provides you with a foundation for asking for your action step or readjusting your objective.

"Checking is your compass for staying on course."

☑ Don't negotiate too early

Selling and negotiating are separate phases of the sales process. Selling is the phase in which you determine if the customer wants to do business with you and/or you want to do business with the customer. You identify customer needs, build trust, and show the value you bring in meeting customer needs. Negotiating is the phase in which price, terms, and profit are determined.

Any time you are discussing price or terms, you have moved into the negotiating phase of the call. In the negotiating phase, people are afraid of being taken and, therefore, can feel defensive. During negotiation, it is usually too late to identify needs, build trust, or gather the kind of key information that would have been readily available in the selling phase.

It is fairly common for a customer *early* in the selling phase to say, "Just tell me a price before anything else." Before discussing price or terms, ask yourself two questions. Do you know the customer's needs? Does the customer know the value you bring to the table?

If the answer to either question is no, hold off. But don't say no. Say, "Yes, so we can discuss price, may I ask a few questions and get the details I need?" If a customer won't give you information, it is risky for you to give pricing, either specific or ballpark. Instead, remain consultative and repeat your need for information. If the customer wants pricing information early in the sales process, start the trading process by trading price information for customer information. Unless you understand needs, you won't be able to connect price or terms with value to the customer.

Avoid negotiating until you understand the customer's needs and you have shown your value. Make sure you are ready to negotiate: know needs and position value before getting to price or terms.

If the customer makes demands, go beneath the demand to get to the need. Why? Because there is usually only one way to satisfy a demand, but there are multiple ways to satisfy a need.

Use negotiation strategies to preserve your price and terms. Always discuss price or terms in the context of value to the customer.

Finally, remain consultative. Even with an adversarial negotiator, don't become adversarial. You don't have to be adversarial to be in control.

As you negotiate, use the following strategies:

Get to the need beneath the demand: There is usually only one way to satisfy a demand, but there are multiple ways to satisfy a need.

Trade, don't give: When you do make a concession, trade. Keep track of your concessions and make one concession at a time.

Use the power of silence: Once you state price, be silent. The first to speak is usually the first to concede. This is one time not to check for feedback, since a check when you have put price or terms on the table weakens your position. It takes strength, but be silent.

"Knowing when to negotiate helps you know what to negotiate."

☑ *Treat closing as a process*

*T*he sale is measured by the close: the close represents how well you identified and met your customer's needs. Salespeople always want to talk about closing. However, many salespeople are hesitant to close. Some fear being rejected. Others don't want to close down communications. And others don't want to seem pushy.

The one thing that most salespeople who are reluctant to close have in common is they view closing as an all-or-nothing process. They think they have to wait until the end—when everything is at stake. With this approach, the risks are high.

Salespeople who are really good at closing handle it as a process. They are more confident because they approach closing in phases:

- **Phase 1:** They set a measurable objective before the call.
- **Phase 2:** They use checking questions throughout the call to gauge where they are and make adjustments.
- **Phase 3:** They end each call with a specific action step to maintain momentum or ask for the business.

It is up to you to ask for the next step or the business. However, when you listen, question, position to needs, and check, the closing question may become unnecessary, with the customer asking, "How do we get started?" When this does not happen, it is up to you to close.

Your close can be a "next step" action close such as meeting the economic decision maker, scheduling a demo or pilot program, bringing in a specialist, or whatever comes next in the process before you ask for the business or get a signature on a contract.

By setting an objective before each call, you know what you want to achieve by the end of the call. That gives you the focus and guidance to close. Your measurable objective is the action step you want to reach by the end of the call. It helps ensure you maintain momentum and it lets you realistically gauge your success.

Most salespeople go into a call with vague objectives, such as "get closer to the deal." But if you ask yourself, "What will I see at the end of the call?" you can develop measurable, actionable objectives that keep the sale moving.

Checking is a part of the closing process because it gives you a read on how the customer will respond to your close. Before asking for your action step, do a *final check* to find out how the customer feels about what you have discussed relative to satisfying his or her objectives. This final check will pave the way for you to ask for your action step or help you reset your call objective.

If your customer rejects your close, make a second effort. Acknowledge to find out *why* the customer is saying no, address the obstacle, and, as appropriate, close again.

Here's how to be a more effective closer:

Set an objective for each call: To maintain momentum and move the deal forward, make sure the objective is measurable, achievable, and has a time frame.

Check for feedback throughout the call: Ask for feedback on what you position to give you the data and confidence you need to ask for your action step or adjust your call objective.

End each call with an action step: Don't end your call with a vague or indefinite next step. To maintain the momentum, ask for the business or end the call with a concrete next step in place. Get into the habit of asking for an action at the end of each call.

"Develop the habit of closing inch by inch and on the dotted line."

☐ Go it alone

☑ *Leverage all resources*

---

*T*he most effective salespeople have strong relationships with their customers and with their colleagues internally. Especially in complex sales, it is critical to understand and gain access to decision makers and key influencers. It is also important to be able to leverage your team—specialists, senior executives, peers, and support professionals.

Identify who makes the decisions for the customer and who influences them. Learn who has the power. To analyze your customer's decision process, ask questions, observe communication patterns, and get input from all contacts. Develop relationships in your customer's organization high and wide. Ask critical questions about commitment to the initiative and find out who on the customer's team supports or opposes the initiative. Find out who holds the purse strings and identify your champion or coach, as well as any possible nemesis. Build relationships with third-party, outside influencers such as attorneys, auditors, and bankers, as needed.

Leverage your team early in the deal to create internal support so the resources you need are available when you need them. Create positive working relationships with specialists, senior management, or support team members—*before* you need them. Share credit and reciprocate in supporting them.

For example, a well-placed phone call from your senior to a senior in your customer's organization can give you the edge you need to win. One salesperson effectively used a senior manager in his organization to win an important piece of business. He knew his customer would be buying a new system and the situation was very competitive, so he sought the support of his treasurer, who had a good relationship with the CFO of the customer's organization. The salesperson asked his treasurer to call the CFO and fully prepared him to persuasively tell their story and reinforced the two issues that were most important to the CFO. According to the salesperson, that phone call clinched the sale.

Here are a few ideas to help you leverage all the resources you need to win:

Map your customer's decision-making process: Ask questions, observe, and analyze your customer's decision-making process. Gain access to decision makers. Know who influences your customer.

Enlist the support of your colleagues: Develop credibility internally with your team members. When you win, share credit.

Develop a coach in the customer's organization: Identify and cultivate a respected customer contact who will champion your sale and provide you with invaluable guidance and support to help you win. If you don't have a coach in each of your key relationships, develop one.

"Everyone knows someone. Good salespeople know how to turn 'six degrees of separation' into seven-figure sales."

☑ *Follow up flawlessly*

*F*ollow-up gives salespeople a way to differentiate themselves that is completely within their control. Follow-up is one of the easiest ways to create credibility and trust with a customer: a promise made is a promise kept—on time. Follow-up is needed before the sale, during the sale, after the sale, and even when no deal is on the table.

Many salespeople are average at best at following up. But flawless follow-up can help set you apart. It takes commitment, awareness, and an effective daily to-do system. Write down whatever you commit to on a *daily to-do* and check the list at the start and end of each day. Be fanatical about this. If it is June 2 and you commit to something for June 29, note that on June 29 and also in mid-June as a reminder.

When you get a call from a customer or colleague, call back ASAP, even if it is only to set a time for the full call. Don't let more than 12 hours elapse without a response. Be *more* responsive than your competitors and/or your own colleagues. Check your *voice mail* every *three hours* and update it as necessary.

Most important, follow up when promised—ahead of time is even better. Keep customers posted. If something will be late, call the customer *before* he or she calls you. Alert customers to delays, apologize, and tell specifically what you will do and what the next step will be. Show concern and a sense of urgency. Better yet, don't be late. Keep your commitments! Ask the customer early on what he or she expects, to clarify and help you meet expectations.

Following a sales call, get an e-mail out *quickly* to all decision makers. Tailor it to the needs and questions of the customers. Use voice mail to concisely update or recap next steps and maintain contact.

Use letters as appropriate as covers for proposals, etc.

When a decision is being made, stay close to the customer through phone calls and e-mails and, when appropriate, face to face throughout the decision period. If a deal is pending and you are away, make sure your office can reach you ASAP or is prepared to handle the call on your behalf. Call and e-mail your customers, maintain close contact, and find reasons to stay close during the decision process.

To help you manage all relationships, put active and non-active customers on an appropriate relationship follow-up schedule to avoid the "out of sight out of mind" syndrome. Follow up with customers after meetings, after important events, before and after implementation, and on special occasions (such as to wish them a happy holiday).

Follow up internally to post your colleagues, thank them, and also make sure no one has dropped the ball. Double-check with the customer to gauge satisfaction. Leverage your team (specialists, seniors, assistants).

Ban the words "Let me know ..." and "Call me," from your follow-up language. It is up to you to call your customers and to set specific next steps at the end of each contact.

To follow up to create a winning edge:

Have a system: Keep and use an active daily to-do. Check your to-do to start and end each day.

Have a sense of urgency: Be appropriately relentless in getting things done. Communicate this commitment to your customers.

Keep follow-up in your court: Don't expect your customers to do your job.

"One of the best follow-up calls is the thank-you call. A 'thank you for the meeting' call can lead to a 'thank you for the business' call."

☑ *Validate the opportunity*

Many salespeople trust their instincts about whether or not they have a real, qualified opportunity. As helpful as "gut" feelings are, the best information must come from the key source—the customer. As logical as this sounds, it is surprising how many times salespeople guide their deals by making assumptions and using information they've gotten primarily from themselves.

There are critical, tough questions that must be answered by customers: "What is the customer's most compelling need?" "What is driving the opportunity?" "What is the time frame?" "Is there a compelling event?" "What budget has been allocated to the initiative?" "What is the decision criterion?" "Who are the competitors?" "How do I rank?" "What value do I bring?" "What is my relationship?" "What is my level of access to the decision makers?" "How does the customer perceive my value and differentiation compared to my competitors?"

Salespeople make three classic mistakes in qualifying and assessing opportunities:

- They assume that they know the answers to vital questions.
- They forget that deals change daily based on internal customer changes and the competitive landscape and they don't change their message and strategy.
- They validate, they do it one time with one person.

Some salespeople delude themselves into thinking there is an opportunity when there is none. Others may assume they don't have a chance when, in fact, they could win. Without validation, it is all guesswork.

Validation is a perfect blending of six critical skills: presence, relating, questioning, listening, positioning, and—most important—checking. When you are validating, your goal is to understand how customers think and, more important, to drill to a deeper level and find out *why* they feel as they do.

So, for example, you may ask, "Who are the competitors?" but then you may back away from asking the tougher questions about how the customer and each of his or her colleagues feel about your competitors and then how that compares with what the customers think of you.

The answers to validating questions provide an understanding of needs and also the criteria and politics involved in the process of making the decision. Validating gives you the information you need to help you differentiate your message to create a winning solution.

The next time you are in dialogue, really take note of how may times you validate to drill down and confirm information.

To help you validate and gain additional information:

Assume nothing: Double-check all information to make sure it is valid and real.

Remember that things change: Revalidate and adjust your strategy and message.

Don't stop at one: You need more than one perspective to ensure your information is correct.

"Validation is a perfect blending of six critical skills: presence, relating, questioning, listening, positioning, and—most important—checking."

☑ *Make it happen*

*A*s business becomes more complex and competitive, you must become more skilled and strategic. The level of change across the board is unprecedented. There is a feeling in many sectors that in the past decade there was more buying than selling. The focus often was on the product and the transaction, rather than the customer, the value add, and the relationship.

It is up to you to determine if you have kept up with the level of change around you, if you have altered how you sell. Are you actively changing or merely tweaking?

The dialogue possible with sales talk will help you focus on your customers in a new way. It will help you put the customer first and, as one top performer said, "help the customer put you on speed dial!" The objective is to use the dialogue to truly understand your customers' needs, to position compelling, tailored messages that customers see as solutions to their needs, to close, and to deepen relationships.

The six critical skills of presence, relating, questioning, listening, positioning, and checking are at the core of sales talk. These skills are the *tools* that you need from your opening to your close. A weakness in even one skill will hold you back.

Throughout the 20 lessons in this book, there has been a consistent theme that your sale happens in the dialogue and that Sales talk takes two. You have the tools available to you at all times in your skills. Your message and your skills are the hub of your sale. Without them you can't go forward. With them you move to your goal of closed sales and long-term successful relationship.

You are good now. You also know you can be better.

For your next call, select one of the six critical skills to be your focus:

Relate to your customers: Leverage rapport to make customer feel comfortable with you. Use acknowledgment to maintain connection and empathy to create a closer bond.

Ensure your presence: Check the level of interest, energy, and conviction that you project. Show your interest in the customer, not just the sale.

Question, listen, and check: Set a questioning strategy. Ask more questions and position them to gain a full understanding of needs. Listen effectively to the customer's message—words, tone, and pace—and read the body language. Check throughout to elicit feedback and make adjustments.

Position your message: When you understand the customer's needs, position your message to meet those needs and ask for the business.

Identify what has worked for you in the past and improve it so it will work in the future. Know that you sell much more than your product. You, as the "human face" of your company, are the sale and your Sales talk makes it happen.

"For the twenty-first century salesperson-client relationship, the salesperson must shift from the 'expert' to being a 'resource.'"

"By unlearning old product-selling techniques and learning how to engage in a true sales dialogue with your customers, you can increase your sales results and build lasting customer relationships."

"While many salespeople think needs, they talk product, true to the traditional selling formula. Asking questions and listening can change all that."

About the Author

Linda Richardson is the founder and president of Richardson, training consultants to corporations, banks, and investment banks globally. Linda pioneered the concepts of consultative selling and integrated, customized curriculums in the training and development industry. She has designed and implemented customized sales and leadership training systems to provide clients with fully integrated curricula for all levels and departments in their organizations.

Linda is also on the faculty of Wharton School, where since 1989 she has taught relationship selling as an accredited graduate course and where she teaches sales and coaching/management programs for the Wharton Executive Development Center. She is the author of eight books and her most recent books with McGraw-Hill are *Selling by Phone, Stop Telling, Start Selling,* and *Sales Coaching—Making the Great Leap from Sales Manager to Sales Coach.*

Among the clients of Richardson are Federal Express, General Mills, Tiffany & Co., Dell Computer, JP Morgan Chase & Co., Citibank, Standard Chartered, and Chubb Group of Insurance Companies. Richardson has 15 regional offices in the United States and presence in London, Australia, Singapore, Latin America, and Asia.

She is currently on the Mayor's Council for the Arts for the City of Philadelphia. Linda has been featured in *Forbes Magazine, Across the Board,* The Conference Board Magazine, *The Philadelphia Inquirer, Nation's Business, Success Magazine, Selling Magazine,* and *Selling Power Magazine.* Linda provides monthly cyber sales tips through her Web site, **www.richardson.com.**

Other Titles in the McGraw-Hill Professional Education Series

Notes

Notes

The Sales Success Handbook
Order Form

1–99 copies	_____ copies @ $7.95 per book
100–499 copies	_____ copies @ $7.75 per book
500–999 copies	_____ copies @ $7.50 per book
1,000–2,499 copies	_____ copies @ $7.25 per book
2,500–4,999 copies	_____ copies @ $7.00 per book
5,000–9,999 copies	_____ copies @ $6.50 per book
10,000 or more copies	_____ copies @ $6.00 per book

Name _____

Title _____

Organization _____

Phone (_____)_____

Street address _____

City/State (Country) _____ Zip _____

Fax (_____)_____

Purchase order number (if applicable) _____

Applicable sales tax, shipping and handling will be added.

☐ VISA   ☐ MasterCard   ☐ American Express

Account number _____ Exp. date _____

Signature _____

Or call 1-800-842-3075
Corporate, Industry, & Government Sales

The McGraw-Hill Companies, Inc.
2 Penn Plaza
New York, NY 10121